REAL TALK

vol. 1

Straight talk to youths and for youths

By Elijah Hood Jr.

Table of Content

Introduction

First, let me start off by saying, I am not a celebrity, I didn't grow up rich, and I'm not a professor or doctor with several degrees on the wall. I AM YOU! The one that didn't have the best role model to follow. YOU! The one who's self-esteem was not on the level that it should be because of the family environment. YOU! The one that struggled in school because it was hard to focus, with all the other things going on in life. So, as you are reading this book, keep in mind that I can relate whether you are Black, White, Asian or Hispanic; short, tall, fat, or skinny. I encourage you to read this book with an opened mind so you can really absorb the contents of it.

Real Talk (Volume 1) touches on several different aspects of juvenile lives. Many people are dead, in prison, addicted to drugs, etc. due to decisions they made as juveniles. The contents of this book may save a life and/or be the motivation you need to break negative cycles. It might be what you, a friend, or a relative need to work through some struggles that you may be facing at this very moment. Get the book! Read the book! Apply the book! You won't regret it.

Chapter 1 Peer Pressure

They say words can never hurt you, that's not true. No one likes to be called derogatory names {lame, pie, nerd, hoe, etc.} And it's not easy to just ignore names like these. Since we can't control what other people say and do, let's talk a little about ways to recognize when people are using derogatory names to apply peer pressure. You know right from wrong. Knowing that, you know when someone is asking you to do something wrong. So, what happens when a family member or friend tries to get you to go along with them in wrongdoing? {Stealing, fighting, shooting, rape, murder, robbery, drugs, etc.} The first thing that pops in your mind is something you already know, "YOU SHOULD NOT DO IT!!! This is wrong! But what happens to those thoughts? Why do they go away so quickly? PEER PRESSURE!

Take a moment to picture a see-saw. The objective of a seesaw is to move up and down. How you may ask? By fluctuating the weight on both sides. The side that weighs more goes down, while the side that weighs less goes up in the air. Well, the same things happen when your conscience is trying to get you to do what you know is right. Your conscience is Fighting against the peer pressure which is trying to get you to do what you know is wrong. Whichever one is stronger and weighs more heavily on your mind, is probably the one you will choose.

How can you balance things out to where your conscience has a better chance of overcoming the peer pressure? There are several things you can do to help with that. First, you want to recognize when peer pressure exists. Keep in mind that it can come in many ways {family, friends, music, TV, internet, adults, children, girlfriends, boyfriends, etc.} Anything and everything that makes you consider doing something that you know is wrong, can be peer pressure.

Secondly, you want to remember all the consequences of your actions. Not just going to jail, but how long you might be in jail. Not just the possibility of getting shot or shooting someone, but the possibility of getting killed or killing someone. Think about all the people you will hurt verses all the people you will impress. You will hurt and disappoint your parents, grandparents, brothers, sisters, aunts, uncles, cousins, teachers, girlfriends, boyfriends and the list goes on and on.

Who will you impress? Absolutely no one, because peer pressure is not about impressing, it's about power and control. It's about getting you to do something they don't want to do themselves, or something they don't want to do alone. It's about seeing if they can get you to do whatever they want. Think about it this way, if you wanted to pop a balloon, what do you apply? PRESSURE! When squeezing out toothpaste or chewing gum or even pushing a lawn mower, it all takes applied pressure to be successful in getting them to do what you want them to do. That is what some people try to do to you. Unlike those items, you have a mind, heart, and conscience to help you to resist when you know it is the wrong thing to do. I would be lying to you if I said that is easy to walk away, especially when it is someone close to you. But that is why you were born with your own brain, heart, and conscience. It is up to you to use what you were born with to decide whether to say no when it comes to wrong doing or allow others to pressure or persuade you in your decision making.

Another thing to remember is, some people will try to make bad things look fun and cool, to influence you to go along with it. DON'T FALL FOR IT!! Everyone likes to have fun, but you must recognize the differences between "healthy legal fun" and "unhealthy dangerous illegal fun". The best way to do that is to go back to the see-saw method. If the good outweighs the bad, you can do it, but if the bad outweighs the good, don't do it. Life is already short, why do risky things to possibly cut your life even shorter. The end results will never be "fun" instead the outcome may lead you to jail, getting hurt, or even death. So be your own person and recognize peer pressure when it exists. Have a plan in place to fight against peer pressure and use the tools that you were born with to keep peer pressure from pressuring you.

Chapter 2 Sex

The definition of sex by Merriam Webster www.merriam-webster.com/dictionary/sex is: The state of being a male or female (which is your gender, if you are a boy or girl) or physical activity in which people touch other bodies, kiss each other etc., physical activity that is related to and often includes sexual intercourse.

Sexual intercourse is defined this way (1) heterosexual intercourse involving penetration of the vagina by the penis. (2) Intercourse (as anal or oral intercourse) that does not involve penetration of the vagina by the penis www.merriam-webster.com/dictionary/sex. Now that we know what falls under the category of sex, let's discuss some of the Pros and Cons of juveniles engaging in sexual activity. Let's just put it out there. Sex feels good. It is one of the most personal and intimate ways a person can show their love to one another. It is the natural way humans and animals reproduce.

In the same way sex can bring pleasure it can also bring pain. Especially for a person that is not ready for the responsibilities and/or consequences of having sex before they are ready. What does "being ready" mean?

Well before you can answer that you need to know the responsibilities and/or consequences.

Now I'm assuming you are not a medical doctor and you don't have the medical equipment or tests that is needed to check anyone to see if they have an STD (Sexually Transmitted Diseases). That being the case, contracting an STD is a consequence you should be concerned about. HIV, Chlamydia, Genital Herpes, Genital Warts and Gonorrhea are just a few STD's that you must be aware of. There are over twenty types of STD's affecting more than 13 million men and women in the United States (vmm.edu/.../sexually-transmitted) some of which have no known cures.

Before you say, "Well we use condoms" please know the condom may be used during sexual intercourse to REDUCE the probability of pregnancy and spreading sexually transmitted infections (https://en.wikipedia.org/wikw/condom). Please know that the use of a condom may "reduce", but not eliminate. You also need to keep in mind that although a condom is affective in limiting exposure, some disease transmission may occur even with a condom. You have to ask yourself, is that brief moment of pleasure worth the pain, the embarrassment, the cost of doctor's care and medication and life changes you will have to make, even DEATH. My answer would be NO, but only you can answer for yourself. Remember that you will have to LIVE OR DIE with the answer that you made.

Another thing, the finest boy or girl can have an STD and you will not have a "tell tell" sign that will let you know if a person has an STD. Remember lies are easy to tell. So, what's your best bet so far?

Now let's talk about responsibilities of having sex when you are not ready. REPRODUCTION; having a baby, going through an abortion, miscarriage, still birth or even death. Those are things that can happen to you after that brief moment of pleasure. Let's look at having a baby. How much money do you have saved up? The average cost of raising a child born in 2013 to the age 18 for a middle-income family in the U.S. is approximately $245,340 - $304,480. What if your child was born with a birth defect or mental illness? Are you mentally, physically, and financially ready to deal with that?

What about Abortions? Some of the side effects and risk are heavy or persistent bleeding, infection or sepsis, damage to the cervix, damage to other organs even death all for a brief moment of pleasure. That's just some of the physical things you will have to deal with as a pregnant female who decides to have an abortion. Emotionally, you may have to deal with regret, guilt insomnia, relationship issues, suicidal thoughts, feeling of depression, and eating disorders all for a brief moment of pleasure. I'm not saying that all these things will definitely happen to you, but the possibilities and risks involved carries a lot of weight "See-Saw". Even though the emotional affects appear to be just for females, males can also experience post-abortion trauma.

The points to remember are that you are too young, inexperienced, and unprepared to be dealing with the responsibilities and consequences of sexual activities. So why put yourself in that position for a brief moment of pleasure? It's Not Worth It! As juveniles you tend to focus on the "here and now", which would be that moment of pleasure, but as difficult as it may be and as un cool as it may seem, you must think about your future.

Think about it! When you wake up, you think about what to wear, what you're going to eat, and what you're going to do no matter if it's good, bad, or ugly. You think about those things because it becomes natural. That is how you need to be when it comes to decisions. If you were having a hard time deciding what to wear, you wouldn't just go out naked or go out wearing the first thing you come across. Why? Because you will consider the consequences. People might laugh and tease you; you will feel embarrassed and ashamed. That's why you would think, then make the rights decision based off what you think the consequences might be. Apply that same thought process when it comes to sex. Unlike a bad outfit, sex can lead to much worse consequences. Besides that, ask yourself what is the big rush? Why is it that young people, like me, are out here doing things that can destroy all their future plans?

Knowing the consequences, why do people continue to do it? Two reasons, (1) young people look at the development of their bodies instead of the development of their brains. Boys feel that if they can get an erection, growing pubic hairs, or know the basics when it comes to sexual activity, they are ready to have sex. Girls feel that once their breast and butt start developing and start having interest in boys, they are ready to have sex. That is not call "ready to have sex" – it's called puberty. Puberty is the physical changes every boy and girl go through, but we don't think and make decisions with the physical parts of our body, we make decisions and think with the mental parts of our body, specifically the brain.

The parts of the brain that involves the ability to get you thinking about future consequences resulting from current actions is call the frontal lobe {Wikipedia.org}. It can take up until your late 20s for your frontal lobe to reach full maturity. In other words, even though a teenager might be physically ready for sexual activity, since their brains are not on the same level of maturity, they are not ready. Teenagers have been going off of their physical development more so than their mental development, which have brought forth disastrous results for many young ones today.

Secondly, sex is looked at as the cool thing to do, a trend. Something that you do if you are cool and not do if you're lame. That's your body, your future, so regardless of what others say, if you know that you are not ready, DONT FALL FOR IT!! You would be the one who must deal with the consequences. So, do not use your body like a cell phone or pair of shoes. Because just like a cell phone and pair of shoes, if you abuse it and use it the wrong way it won't last very long.

Chapter 3 Education

I didn't like school. It wasn't the educational aspect of school as to why I disliked school, it was the many things I was dealing with. It was the problem and issues that I had at home with my family. My self-esteem was not where it should have been. I had difficulties focusing on what the teacher was saying. I had no one to talk to about my problems or issues. Although I didn't bother anyone, however, if you messed with me all the frustration that I had built-up came out on you. I didn't know how to love because I never felt love. I had all these problems and issues, but I was expected to go to school and focus on getting a good education. Some people are strong enough to do that, but I wasn't.

The problem with not being able to fight through all the adversities that you may be feeling in order to get your education, is that in the end, your situation will be worse. Think about it, you might have one or both parents that may be in prison, on drugs, dead, or just plain neglectful when it comes to the responsibilities of being a parent. Whatever the reasons are, it is making your life as a child even more difficult than it has to be.

Here is where you come in, you have the option of working harder now to make things much easier in adulthood or taking it easy now and make life much harder in adulthood. Before you make that decision, you must understand that responsibilities multiply as you get older. Right now, you might have your phone bill, you might have to purchase some of your own clothing or food. But as an adult, you and only you are responsible for transportation, a place to live, food to eat, clothes to wear, utilities needed in the home {electricity, water, gas, cable, phone etc.} Let's not forget about insurance such as dental, health, vision, life, auto, home, etc. Then there are items you take for granted like soap, toilet paper, toothpaste, deodorant, detergent, lotion etc. If you decide to have children, you will have the responsibility of providing these things for them as well.

Imagine you having to deal with all of the things you're facing now on top of all the responsibilities of an adult. That can be overwhelming for the strongest person. You may be asking, what does that have to do with me getting a good education? The obvious is that educated people can make more money instead of being unhappy with a job they don't like. A good education allows you to work in a field that you enjoy. Getting a good education gives you a sense of accomplishment and fulfillment with your self-esteem. A good education will open doors to goals and dreams you may have, like being a professional athlete, an actor or actress, a doctor or lawyer, or even a judge or the president of the United States. Whatever it is you want to be, starts right here right now with your education.

I would be lying if I told you that money and education will solve all of your problems. In an imperfect world filled with imperfect people, it is impossible to solve all the problems of everyone. Knowing that, you're not trying to solve all of your problems, but would you like to solve some them by working hard and staying focused and getting a good education. Those are a few things that would help you do that.

Think about it this way, if you were a guest on a game show and had the options of winning $100 for doing 10 push-ups or $100,000 for doing 50 push-ups which one are you going for? More than likely you would go for the $100,000 even though the 50 push-ups would be harder for you to do and take longer for you to get to. You still would go for it because of the end result which would be a prize that is much more rewarding. The same is true when it comes to your education. You can skip school, horseplay, get kicked out in the name of having fun {the $100 prize}. Or you can work hard, focus on getting good grades and a good education which will be harder for you and may take a little longer to get to. However, as a result, you will be able to enjoy things like that car you like, the house you desire, helping others, providing a better life for your family {that big prize of $100,000}.

I'm not saying that you cannot have those things without a good education, but it will be easier for you in life with an education than without it. Education opens doors to a better life like that. Lack of education closes doors. Either way you will have to pass through those doors as you go through life. So why not work to have those doors open to better your chances of having a happier life, even if it is not so happy right now. The first step is to GET YOUR EDUCATION.

Chapter 4 Balance

The definition of the word balance is "an even distribution of weight enabling someone or something to remain upright and steady". Synonyms for the word balance are stability and steadiness. When you think about your life as it is right now, can you honestly say that your life is balanced? Do you have both of your parents living with you right now? Do you get the proper food and health care that you need? Are you rewarded and commended when you do good things? Are you counseled and held responsible for things you do wrong? Are your parents actively involved in your life when it comes to your education, friends, and any extra curricula activities? These are some of the things that make a balanced life. Sad to say but most of you that is reading this book don't have these things.

Just know that you are not alone, and all is not lost. You are just going to have to put in a little more work on your end to balance out what someone else might have dropped the ball on. How do you do that? First, you need to figure out what you need more of and less of in your life. As a young person, that can be difficult, but it is necessary in order to minimize the mistakes you make in life. A lot of girls tend to fall in the arms of males that have nothing but bad intentions for them, all because they are lacking something. A lot of boys tend to act out or attach themselves to groups, all because they are lacking something. That is what an unbalanced life will cause you to do.

For example, let's say you wanted to make some chocolate chip cookies. The basic things you will need are eggs, flour, butter, etc. What if you didn't have flour? Would you just throw a cup of dirt in there? What if you had no chocolate chips? Would you just throw some small rocks in there? I'm sure your answer is "no way". Well that is exactly what you are doing with your life right now. If mom and dad are not doing what they are supposed to be doing, you are plugging in the first thing you can find to fill that hole instead of seeking out what you are truly missing from your life.

We learned as toddlers that you cannot put a square piece in where only a triangle piece fit. So, no matter how many boys or girls you choose to deal with and no matter what gang or click you choose to join, it will not be a match for the empty spot in your life right now. Your mother and father will always be your parents. You don't need new parent in order to fill that spot, but you do need a positive adult role model. A person that will display examples of good values, positive attitude, and behavior. Someone that will help guide you through the struggles of your teenage years. There is nothing wrong with having someone like that in addition to having your mom and dad.

As humans, it is natural for us to have cravings. When we are thirsty, we crave liquid. When we are hungry, we crave food. Well, we also crave things like guidance, love, support, structure, and balance. What you are doing to yourself is equivalent to drinking gasoline to satisfy your thirst. Yes, it is a liquid, but a liquid that will cause you pain and not joy. You have had enough pain in your life already. So instead of more pain, let's see how you can balance your life with more joy.

There are several groups and youth organizations out there just waiting to help a young one like yourself. Big Brothers & Sisters of America, The Boys & Girls Aid Society, Strong Women Strong Girls, Boy scouts of America, and the list goes on and on. It might even be someone in your family or school that might be perfect for that spot. Just remember, that person or group needs to have the qualities to help you balance your life, not hurt you. Once you do that, you will soon see and feel your life balancing out.

Chapter 5 Real (Truth) 100%

The word real is defined as actually existing as a thing or occurring in fact; not imagined or supposed. Now, you have heard the term "keeping it real" or "keeping it 100%", keep that term in mind when answering this question. How much of the music that you listen to or movies that you watch are base off 100% truth? Before you answer, understand that music {Rap, R&B, Rock, Country, etc.} and movies {action, comedy, mystery, horror, etc.} are parts of the billion-dollar entertainment industry also known as show business. The primary responsibility of this industry is to "entertain". How do they do that? Simple, they find out what you like then sell it to you. Not what you need, just what you like. Is there anything really wrong with that? Not at all, the problem comes in when people like yourself take these movies and music—which is only meant for your entertainment—and start to implement them into your everyday lives.

It is not entertaining to hear the negative, humiliating things that happens in prison or how important it is to get a good education. It is hard to do modern day dances at parties or clubs with lyrics about being respectful and helping others. Let's be 100%, that won't sell. Not only that, what rapper you know will make music about how they were sexually assaulted, beat up or had to pay for their safety while locked up? Would you? That is why it is very important to separate the world of entertainment from the real world that you are living in.

When the entertainment world makes music or movies about shooting, doing drugs, hitting licks or murder, they can make money. When you do these things in real life, you will end up dead or in prison. That's real, that's keeping it 100%.

In order to rap, you need to know how to read. In order to sign a deal, you need to know how to read and understand all the details of your contract. Do you think that all these entertainers were born with the ability to do those things? They had to get their education and some of them continued their education by going to college. Don't be fooled by the stories that you hear. That goes for the entertainment industry and the people around you. Yes, the people around you.

I am sure that you have heard the stories about how they were running things while they were locked up, how nobody tried them, how they beat up this person or shanked that person. Not true, nor is it fun and easy robbing people or breaking in houses. You might laugh if you get away with it, but what if you don't? What if you or your friend get shot in self defense during the robbery? No Fun! What if a neighbor or silent alarm alerts the police while you are breaking in the house and you get caught? No Fun! What if you are shooting at someone and kill them or an innocent bystander? Now you are facing murder charges. No Fun, right? Those things happen and can happen to you.

There is not a person sitting in prison, jail, detention center or the grave that would tell you "if I had a chance to do it all over again, I would do the same thing" because they wouldn't. However, by then, it is too late for some of them. Don't make the same mistakes many have made by believing really good stories instead of the real truth.

Chapter 6 Think

There are at least fifty states in the United States, (48) are continental (all together) and Hawaii and Alaska are the other two. There are over 20,000 cities in the United States, so just imagine how many communities or neighborhoods there are in the United States, in the world. Now answer this question and take all the time you need to think before you answer. How many of those neighborhoods do you or your family own? Let me answer that for you, NONE. So why you are so willing to fight, shoot, even kill for something that never was and never will be yours? I know that you might be saying that it is not about the actual neighborhood, but more about the people in the neighborhood and respect.

Let's talk about the people in your neighborhood for a minute. Do you even know all the people in your neighborhood? More than likely, you do not. Like most people, you only know a few which are the ones you or your family members associate with. So, is it the neighborhood that you are trying to protect or represent? Or could it be that you are caught up following a small group of people within your neighborhood? Small groups that are into doing things that you know are wrong, but you are going along to get along.

I can guarantee you without even stepping one foot in your neighborhood, that more people in your "hood" are against the violence, drug activity, gang activity, etc. then there are that approve of it. That being the case, it cannot be about the neighborhood or the respect of the people? So, what is it then? Is it the set you claim (gang in which you are affiliated with)? If so, think about what you are doing. You want nothing to do with the groups of people in other gangs or "hoods". You are willing to fight, shoot, or even kill those people. You don't want to live by them, play with them, and not even speak to them unless you have a reason to. You feel like you are better than them, harder than them, and cooler than them. No one in your family or neighborhood are allowed to associate with them or that is a violation. Sounds about right?

All of these feelings that you have for this other group of people that you really don't know because of a "COLOR" {red, black, blue, brown, etc...} Tell me, what does this remind you of? The racism, hatred, torture, abuse, that people had to endure and fight through in order for you to have the rights in which you have today.

You are continuing the same negative and destructive behavior within your own community, amongst your own people that you wouldn't stand for if it came from someone of a different race or ethnicity.

This is not about respect, this is not about color, and it is surely not about neighborhoods. It is about the one who is reading this book right now. Yes you! For whatever reason you are willing to attach yourself to this small group of people that is hell bent on doing wrong, that's until they get caught. Then suddenly you want to do the right, you want to help keep your little brothers and sisters from following in your footsteps, you're praying every night for your freedom and your family's safety. Why not do that when you are free? Does it makes sense for (your brothers and sisters) to do right because you (the one doing wrong) told them to. That's the point I was trying to make. Not when you "THINK" about it.

Chapter 7 Your Actions

When you are locked up, it's always someone else fault. The police, because he/she arrested you for nothing. The judge, because he/she could have let you go home. The district attorney and probation officer, because they lied on you and requested that the judge keep you locked up. Your parents, because they told the judge that they are having problems with you at home. In your mind, it is everyone else fault you are in the position you are in, but yours.

Out of all the people that you are blaming for your present situation, which one of them forced you to take the actions that landed you in trouble? Your parents may not be setting the best examples, you may not live in the safest and positive environment, your siblings and friends may not be the best role model to follow. Although these are influences, negative influences, but still influences.

The word influences are defined as "the ability to have an effect on the character, development, or behavior on someone, something, or yourself." Nowhere in the definition of this word does it say that a person is being forced or made to do anything. So even when you have negative influences in your life, it is still ultimately up to "YOU", when it comes to the actions "YOU" decide to take. When "YOU" break in a house, "YOU" are using your two feet and your two hands. When "YOU" are shooting at someone or robbing someone "YOU" are using your trigger finger. When "YOU" are out there wilding out, having fun getting away with illegal things, you are not blaming anyone then. It is only when you get caught up, that's when the blame game starts.

Bad decision making trying to build up your street credit, is not due to anyone else. It is about you and your common sense—good sense and sound judgment in practical matters. Most young people like yourself allow influences from others to dictate your actions more so than common sense. Doing so results in trouble. That is why it is important to remember that the consequences of your actions will be on you. So, accept that "YOU" control your movements, your decision making, and your actions.

Chapter 8 Fortitude

Everyday living can be very hard. Being broke is hard, being hungry is hard, doing the right thing is hard, and school is hard. I can go on and on, but I think you get the point. Since we can't change life and the hard facts of it, how do we deal with the pains and adversities that come with life? That's where the word fortitude comes in.

Fortitude is another word for courage, endurance, and strength. You must have fortitude when living your life. Everyone has problems. It doesn't matter if you're rich, poor, black, white, short, tall, girl or boy at a point in your life, you will have to work through problems. How do you think the singers and rappers you like made it to where they are now? FORTITUDE! How do you think the athletes you like made it to where they are now? FORTITUDE! How do you think those people made it to this day? Well think of it this way, you weren't born with the ability to walk and talk, read and write. That took fortitude.

Somewhere along your journey in life, you lost your fortitude and started looking for the easy ways out.

The problem is, there are no easy ways out of hard situations. People might tell you that there are, but realistically there's not. When you hear people make that statement just know they are lying to you. Sure, you can steal, rob, or sell drugs to get money instead of working, but when you get caught {not if, but when} you will be doing "hard" time. Sure, you can skip school, drop out instead of getting a good education, but when it's time to get out and take care of you and your own family, getting the best job to support you all will be much "harder". So, as you can see, you can't get around going through "hard" times and situations. You can only turn hard into harder because things get harder as you get older. Think twice before "working easy" to make life much harder later in life. Doesn't it make more sense to work harder now for your life to be much easier in the future. In order to do this, you must regain your fortitude.

Start with small things like saying please and thank you. Hopefully, that will lead to bigger things like doing your homework and cleaning up after yourself. Eventually, you will find yourself overcoming big challenges like reframing from engaging in wrong doings and illegal activities. This is not an overnight process. Let's compare it to exercise. No one starts off with big muscles. A person may start off with five or ten pushups, then keep working on it by gradually increasing the amount until he/she has reached their goals. Just like those pushups, it will be hard in the beginning, but your fortitude and muscles will respond the same by getting stronger as you go on. Keep in mind that "hard" now makes it "easy" later and one of the main ingredients is fortitude. I promise you that you won't regret it.

Chapter 9 You Do the Math

Have you ever heard people say things like, "what comes around goes around" or "two wrongs don't make a right?" Well some people call those sayings cliché. Cliché is a saying that is used over and over and betrays a lack of original thought. Some people strongly believe in clichés like these and live their lives by rules that supports them. Regardless to whether you believe clichés or not, some things that we do and some decisions that we make have inevitable results – they are certain to happen.

If you are sitting in a detention facility, jail, or prison, I want you to look back on your life. Reflect on all the times you got away with doing the wrong thing. Think about the chances you were given, the warnings and advice you ignored. Now you are sitting in a room or a cell mad at the world because you might spend your birthday locked up, miss your favorite holidays, sporting events, movies among with other things that a young adult enjoys . Your girlfriend or boyfriend is moving on, family members and friends dying, and you can't be there to comfort them. You are in your feelings because all those things are happening, and you can't do anything about it. WHAT DO YOU EXPECT? Life don't stand still while you are locked up. If you're going to be mad, then be mad at yourself for continuing to do wrong and expecting the end results to be good.

Life doesn't work that way, no one is perfect nor is anyone asking you to be. People make bad decisions and mistakes all the time but continuing doing wrong {illegal activities} is not a mistake or bad decision. It's a continued bad behavior that will only result in corrupt things for you. Wrong will not equal right no matter how you justify it. You may think it does because at some point it may appear that you are getting away with it, but that's just a mirage. A mirage is an optical illusion, something that appears real or possible but it's not.

I know that some of you may be thinking "every time I try to do right and stay out of trouble, bad things still happen to me". First of all, be real with yourself. You know your true motive better than anyone else. You know if you were really trying to be good and stay out of trouble. Or if you're just being deceptive by making things appear different from the truth. Nevertheless, let's say that you are doing right, just know that good results will eventually start happening. Don't expect your life to magically change from bad to great overnight, but trust that it will produce good results.

One thing that you can do to help you continue to do well is to surround yourself with people that are trying to do the same. Think about it this way! If you and your friends decided to get in a car and drive to the mall, you're the only one in the car that has showered within the last week. The other guys stink, and I mean really stink, lol. The longer you sit in that car with them, what do you think will happen? The stronger smell will eventually over power the weaker one and rub off on you. Now replace the word smell with good behavior and the same will be true. Surrounding yourself with people that are trying to do good, even though you're not quite there yet, eventually it will motivate you to do the same. Whatever you decide to do, first do the math {BAD + BAD = VERY BAD} and {GOOD + GOOD = VERY GOOD} everyDee's time.

Chapter 10 Wisdom Vs Skills

When you look at adults like your parents, teachers, and guards you are probably thinking that they don't understand what you have been through. They have no idea how it is out here in these streets today; they had it easy; or they can't relate to my story. First of all, don't assume anything about anybody. I know you've heard that old saying "you can't judge a book by its cover". That includes your parents, teachers, and guards. Just like they may not know your story, you don't know theirs. You just assume certain things because of the way a person dress, the jobs they have, or how they carry themselves. What you see now is the person they have become, not where they have been.

With that being said let's discuss some of the stages in life they may have been through. They were born, learned how to talk, read, and write as time went on. More years went by, they went to school, survived through puberty and the physical and emotional changes that comes with it. During these times, they were faced with peer pressure, bullies, problems at home, school, and other adversities that teenage boys and girls go through. The adults that you see now may have been through that and more. They have made mistakes that you have yet to face. They have corrected their faults and learned from them.

That knowledge and experience is what gives adults the quality of WISDOM. You cannot have wisdom without experience and knowledge. Wisdom is a great quality to have. It keeps you from making future mistakes and bad decisions. Wisdom is also a great tool to use when helping friends and love ones with their journey in life. That's where you come in. What you think is wisdom is actually skills {the ability to do something well}. Just because you know about life, doesn't mean you know how to work your way through the challenges of it.

Think about it this way! Let's say you know how to drive. You have a driver's license and the skills that you need to operate any motor vehicle. One day its required that you drive to places that you have never been, in a part of the region you know nothing about. You have no maps, apps, or directions of any kind. Without any assistance to get somewhere that you have never been, it's safe to say that you will be lost. Well, life is very similar to that road trip. Adults having already been through what you are going through now. They have the maps {wisdom} that you need to prevent from getting lost. You have the skills to go through life, but without the needed maps, you are sure to find yourself lost on more than one occasion.

Adults have been teenagers and made it through. You have never been an adult and you are not finish with being a teenager. This being the case, who do you think is in a better position to help prevent the other person from making major mistakes? The adults of course, in order for you to truly benefit from the wisdom {life's map} you must first realize and accept the fact that they understand a lot of what you are going through. They know what's going on in these streets today; they did not have it as easy as you think; and they can relate to your story. Once you realize that, you are more likely to listen and accept the advice that they give you. Remember, it's never too late to ask an adult for advice.

So, you may be locked up right now, suspended from school, put out the house, or just simply lost. Don't just wonder around aimlessly. Do the same thing you would do if you were lost on that road trip. STOP WHAT

YOU ARE DOING! GET DIRECTIONS ON THE RIGHT WAY TO GO! MAKE WHATEVER CHANGES NEEDED AND START IN THAT DIRECTION IMMEDIATELY! With your skills and the right adult's wisdom, you can go as far as you want to go.

Chapter 11 Ride or Die

We're always using the phrase "ride or die" when referring to our friends, homeboys, home girls, our boyfriends and girlfriends, and ourselves. Are you really in the position to ride or die with anyone? Being a ride or die means you will be down with that person no matter what. Through the good, bad, and ugly. You can't be that for anyone when you continue to get locked up or ducking and dodging the police and street rivals.

The phrase "ride or die" was originally pertaining to a female supporting and standing by her man during any times or any activities. Think about that for a second, what female or male has been supporting you and standing by you from day one? When you couldn't do for yourself or when you didn't know what money was. When you needed food or shelter, they fed you and gave you a place to lay your head. They were there to check you when you were wrong and support you when you were right. When you couldn't talk, they were there to talk for you. When you couldn't walk or cloth yourself, they carried you and clothed you. He or she finds a way to come see you on visitation days, change their schedule to be by your side on your court days. Who does that sound like to you? Not your homeboys and home girls.

You can't say all those things about your girlfriends and boyfriends. Those things can only apply to mom, dad, grandparents, aunts, uncles, big brother or sisters. The same people that you take for granted, lie to, disrespect, and disobey, until they are literally burnt out and don't know what else they can do to help you and prevent you from destroying your life. Those are your true ride or die people.

The thing you must keep in mind is that ride or die feelings are based off help, not hurt. I'm not a ride or die if I encourage and support you in doing something that I know will hurt you. How many of the people that you consider to be your "ride or die" have tried to get you to NOT do what you did that landed you in trouble? How many of them are writing you about ways to prevent getting in trouble when you're locked up? How many are there for your love ones while you're locked up, trying to help them? Name the ones that even offered your mom a ride to come visit you or offered to come to court on your behalf. How many names have you come up with so far? Not many, if any, but don't feel bad about that because you are not alone.

Now that you know what being a true ride or die consist of, make the changes in your life now. It's ok to have cordial friends that do not fall under the "ride or die" category, but your loyalty, respect, and trust should be with your true ride or die people. That may just be one person, or it may be several, however many it is, whomever it may be, value them and be there for them as you want and expect them to be there for you.

Chapter 12 Serenity

It is so hard growing up these days. You have to deal with so much. It's like you're damned if you do and damned if you don't. If you go to school and make good grades, stay out of trouble, refrain from any drugs or illegal activities, you will make your parents happy, but you might catch hell with the people in your neighborhood and at school. However, if you do the opposite, you will be in good with your peers, but you will disappoint your parents. Then it will lead to you destroying your future and risk getting in legal trouble.

What do you do? First, you must decide what is most important to you. You don't owe the people at your school anything and they don't owe you anything either. You all just happen to be zoned in the same school district. So, if a friendship develops while you are going to school together, great! If it doesn't, oh well, it's not the end of the world. As far as the people in your neighborhood, if you find a likeminded friend in your neighborhood while living there, great! If not, oh well again, it's not the end of the world.

You must remember, you will not be going to that same school or living in that same neighborhood forever. So, it wouldn't be smart to risk so much by attempting to get in good with people that will only be in your life for a temporary time. I know that it is easier said than done, especially during teenage years. It's natural for you to want to be liked, to want to be in with the cool crowd, to not be picked on, or be alone. That's where the word serenity comes in. Serenity is defined as being untroubled, being in a peaceful state or being calm. Ask yourself, how can I become untroubled with not being in good with the cool crowd? Or remain calm when catching hell from peers for doing the right thing? It's not a cut and dry solution or easy answer to those questions, because what works for one doesn't necessary works for the other.

One way would be to find out what else would make you "in good"? Maybe a skill or talent like sports, music, acting, playing in the band, etc. Talent brings admiration, and admiration bring "cool points" get it? If your talent is more so science fiction, video games, or just reading books then find likeminded people and be "in good" with them. You can't please everyone, and everyone will not like you. With that being said, as long as you have a place to go to, things to do, and people to do it with, serenity will allow your life to be balanced. You will have that untroubled emotional state that you need when faced with the difficult situations you're forced to deal with at school or in your neighborhood.

Just remember, no matter what your likes and dislikes are, what you look like, and what you can or cannot do there is always someone out there that's looking for a friend just like you. The problem may be, they're waiting on that friend to come knocking at their door, put in that friend request, just like you are. In order to develop that healthy state of serenity in your life, you might have to come out of your comfort zone a little bit and put in a little extra work. In the end you will be helping yourself and someone else find serenity.

Chapter 13 Break the Cycle

It's hard to change habits, dysfunctions and unhealthy behaviors that you've been around all your life. Hundreds, if not thousands of people find themselves in and out of jail or dead from following their family cycle. My grandfather sold drugs; my father sold drugs so I will do the same. My grandmother was a thief, my mom is a thief, so I will be a thief too. These are some of the negative cycles that many young ones find themselves feeling trapped in. The problems with following negative cycles like these, you make your life ten times harder than it could be. You're not giving yourself a chance to reach your highest potential. Instead of you writing your own ticket to success in life or lack thereof, you are following the same life mistakes as someone else.

Look at it this way, if your grandparent died after drinking from this bottle with no label, then your parents drank from the same bottle and suffered the same results, are you going to drink from that bottle? No, because you have not only seen the results of drinking from that bottle, but you know that no matter how thirsty you may be, this is not the answer. The same thought process should be applied when you need money and material things. Life is hard and in life situations change for the good and the bad. Just like you wouldn't repeat what your love ones did in the illustration, you shouldn't repeat any dysfunctional and unhealthy behaviors your love ones might be practicing.

Don't allow the bad habits and practices to determine how your life ends up. Just because your parent did it, doesn't make it right. Just because your friends got away with it doesn't mean you will. Just because someone you know have been doing it for years doesn't mean you won't get busted on your very first time. Just because you got away with it before, doesn't mean your younger brother or sister will get away with. BREAK THE CYCLE!

Breaking the cycle is not only beneficial for you, but it also gives the people that came in this world after you a positive example to follow, and the ones before you a reason to make positive changes. Breaking the family cycle does not mean that your parents are bad, it means that somewhere during their life time they picked up some bad habits or learned some unhealthy behaviors that they thought was normal. Or maybe they were not strong enough to break away from those habits or unhealthy behaviors.

These habits can range from drinking, smoking, drug abuse, to physical and emotional abuse, and other criminal activities. Whatever it may be, you need to make it your goal to break the negative cycles. If you have ever been forced to deal with the consequences of bad habits and unhealthy behaviors, you know that it most certainly did not feel like love. Why would you want to make someone that you care about feel the same way? You wouldn't! That is why it's important to start now, while you're young.

If your pants are not fitting right, you would make the proper adjustments. If your hair is not looking right, you would make the proper adjustments. Just like those pants and your hair, adjust your life because things are not right. Break those negative cycles and start new positive cycles for yourself and the ones you love.

Chapter 14 For the Boys

YOUNG MEN!! Please pay attention to what you are about to read. Being a man or a boy is not determined by how many babies you can bring into this world, or how many females you can have sex with. Nor is it determined by how big and bad you think you are. Being a man involves a combination of age and maturity.

"AGE" a legal adult's range between 18-21 years old. If you are too young to engage in a contract like an apartment lease, auto loan, or credit card, etc. YOU ARE NOT AN ADULT! If you are too young to legally purchase a fire arm, legally get your utilities in your name, in your own house, YOU ARE NOT AN ADULT. If you can legally do all those things, then you are at least half ½ of a man.

Now let's talk about the other half. "MATURITY" maturity can be defined differently depending on what you are talking about. We are going to talk about emotional and social maturity. Your emotional and social maturities are determining factors to whether you are a man or not.

Emotional maturity is all about how you understand and manage your emotions. How do you respond to incidents that makes you upset? How do you deal with life's adversities? What do you do when you don't get your way, or someone tell you no? Your answers to these questions help determine your maturity level.

Think about the way you interact with family and friends; the way you interact with adults and elderly people. Can you honestly say that you carry yourself as an adult in these instances? Don't get your physical maturity level confused with emotional and social maturity. You may have hair growing on your face and your chest, you may have the physical features of a man, you may even be sexually active and have a few dollars in your pocket, but none of those things makes you a man. There are a lot of people walking around today that have the age and physical appearance of men, but they lack the most important parts, the emotional and social maturity.

I'm sure you have witnessed people being disrespectful and defiant, all because they feel that they are grown. First, it doesn't matter if you are five or fifty, respect is earned not demanded. Secondly, you don't have to use words to demand that respect. Your maturity, the way you carry yourself, will demand the respect for you. The more responsible and respectful that you are towards yourself and others, the more respect you will demand. But it goes both ways. If you show little to no responsibility and respect, you can expect to get little to no respect from others. This is not easy nor is it an overnight process, but it is something that a man will be willing to do.

It starts by being the best juvenile that you can be. You can't skip from a baby to an adult, it just doesn't work that way. Think about it this way, if you were promoted to 12th grade soon after you graduated Pre School, how do you think you would do? Unless you were some sort of supernatural genius, you would fail miserably. You need those gradual steps from the first through the 11th grade to prepare you for the 12th grade, right? The same is true when it comes to becoming a man, trying to jump to manhood without taking the gradual important steps needed to succeed, will have you destined to fail.

Learn as much as you can while you are a child. Practice the characteristics of a mature man while you are young. That way, when you do reach adulthood, you will be more than ready to take on the responsibilities that come with that title. Until then, be a child, stay in a child's place. Remember, there is nothing wrong with acting your age.

Chapter 15 For the Girls

YOUNG WOMEN!!! Please pay attention to what you are about to read. Being a "thot" is not a career choice. Allowing yourself to be called a bitch (female dog), acting like a bitch (female dog) is not cool. Allowing your body to be tossed around from male to male and treated like a piece of meat is not cute or healthy. Whatever you think that you are getting from this type of behavior, you are going by it the wrong way. Something is wrong in your life and in order to make it right, you must first admit that something is in fact wrong and the behavior that you are displaying is not making it right.

There are several different reasons why young girls display negative behaviors like these. It can range from trying to fit in or dealing with sexual abuse. Whatever the reasons might be, trust me when I say this, "you are only making your situation worse." If you are dealing with low self esteem or some type of emotional trauma, there is help available for you. I know it may be difficult to trust someone at this point but allowing people to take advantage of you or acting out is not going to build your trust with anyone. It's only going to tear you down even more.

When you are emotionally unstable, you can't even trust your own feelings and decision-making ability. That is why it is so important to seek the help that you need. You are not stupid, you peep game, you know right from wrong, you're just in a very vulnerable state and some people are taking advantage of that. Those same people will not be around when you are in your 30's and 40's and dealing with the consequences of the unhealthy behavior. Don't use your body as a treatment for your emotional troubles.

I'm going to let you in on a secret, boys like sex, it's hard for a boy to turn down sex because it's more physical than emotional for them. A horny boy will tell you anything that you want to hear in order to get you to agree to have sex. If you are not in the right state of mind, you will fall for the weakest lines a boy will throw at you. All because what he is saying makes you feel good for that moment. You know that he is telling lies and you know you should disagree with him, but your unstable emotions crave something that will make you feel better. This is the problem; you are satisfying that craving with all the wrong things. When you are thirsty, do you go get a big cup of ice-cold gasoline? No, because you know that gasoline would cause more damage than good. Well the same is true with everything else. Don't attempt to satisfy your natural urge for emotional stability with toxic association and more instability.

Teenage pregnancy, STD's, embarrassment and shameful reputations are just some of the things you will have to deal with in addition to the issues that already exist in your life. Young ladies, stop and take time out now to reevaluate your life. Focus on trying to heal and find healthy more permanent solutions to your problems instead of unhealthy quick fixes.

It doesn't matter what you look like on the outside (big, small, short, tall, dark, light, black, white) don't sell yourself short. Work on raising your self-worth. You cannot change the wrong that someone has done to you, but you can change how you let it affect you. Let your actions command the respect that you deserve. Always remember, you are not a tool or a fool, so don't allow anyone to use you as if you were one.

Chapter 16 Miss Me with That "__ "!

You have every reason not to do right, huh? No, you don't. Those are reasons to fight harder to succeed. But instead of fighting harder to succeed, you change those reasons to excuses to bring up when you are attempting to do illegal things. Yes, it might be more difficult to do right when you feel like you have been wronged.

A difficult childhood can make a person feel cheated in some way. You might have a "don't care" attitude because you have a parent on drugs, in jail, or deceased. You might have had to deal with abuse, abandonment, or some other type of trauma. Whatever the situation you have found yourself in, you can't let it be an excuse for failure.

There are so many men and women with great natural talent that are sitting in prison or jail because they allowed a bad situation to veer them off their path to success. Of course, you have a right to complain and have excuses to quit. But why? What good will either of them do? Remember, life may control the gun, but you hold the bullets. What I mean by that is, you can't control the way life goes sometimes, but you can control how life affects you.

Struggles can make you or break you, so if you are that person with a lot of heart, that person that's not pie or weak, then prove it. Stop using excuses as reasons to not fight through the hard times. If you can talk and walk, then you can work. If you are going to show that you have heart, do it for the right reasons. Don't be in the streets wilding out, trying to impress your peers. Then when you get caught, you begin crying for your mom and praying to be free. That's not heart, that's stupid. You know that eventually you are going to get caught if you are engaging in illegal activities.

Cursing and fighting with parents and siblings, leaving the house and coming back when you feel like it, there is no need in getting upset when all this comes out in court. Why get in your feelings now? If you took half of the energy and smarts that you apply when doing wrong and apply it to doing right, you would see how much better your life would be.

Stop walking around thinking the world owes you something because you have a parent on drugs, dead, locked up or your family is poor. The world doesn't owe you anything, but you owe yourself something. What you may ask? A chance! Yes, a chance to live a normal life. A chance to be happy, a chance to succeed and reach goals that you set. Excuses will not grant you those chances, they will only allow you to add to the things you already have that's veering you off the right path. You don't have to be born rich to become rich, you don't have to be born a success story to become a success story. You just have to start turning your excuses to fail into reasons to succeed. It will not be easy, but that is where you heart comes in. Be hard and have heart, but use that to succeed in life and fight through the difficulties you may be facing in your personal life.

Chapter 17 Hard Work

One fact in life is that you will work hard. The only option that you have when it comes to life and working hard is, whether you want to do it now or later. Before you answer that, I want you to consider a couple things. First, think about your job/responsibilities as a child. Doing well in school, chores around the house, stay out of trouble, that's pretty much it. Now I'm not saying that your job as a child is easy. In fact, some parts of childhood can be quite challenging, but let's compare the responsibilities of a child to those of an adult.

Without a good education or a natural talent, you will be forced to work whatever job you can get to pay your bills. Speaking of bills, you didn't have them as a child, but you do now. Therefore, if you want to take a bath or flush your toilet, you must pay for water. If you want light when it's dark and keep your house and food cool, you will have to pay for electricity. If you plan on watching TV or use the internet, you will have to pay for cable. These are just a few things that you will be responsible for as an adult. As you can see, you will have much more to deal with as an adult verse a child.

Although these are things you will need to have despite your financial situation, there is a lot that you can do while you are young to make your adult life easier. Working hard while in school and getting the best out of your education provides you with more opportunities to get a higher paying job. Doing your chores will teach you good work ethics and how to take pride in the work that you do. Staying out of trouble will help with discipline and restraint needed in adult life. It will also allow you to take advantage of every minute in your childhood to prepare you for adulthood. Business before pleasure should be your frame of mind right now.

No one gets muscle before they lift weights or do pushups. No pain no gain, vegetables before dessert! Why not get the pain out of the way now and work hard to make your life less stressful for when you have the most responsibilities in life? No matter what you want to do in life, it will benefit you more to work now and play later. I'm not saying that you can't have any fun now; however, I am encouraging you to stay focused on the goals that you are trying to reach.

You are young and you should enjoy your youth and the experiences that come with it but be smart when it comes to those life experiences. Don't make bad decisions and take unnecessary risk that will cost you later in life. You might not see all the benefits right now, but trust that making smart choices and staying focused throughout your youth will guarantee that your hard work will pay off. Good things will come to you when you are working hard and doing good things.

Chapter 18 Read! Relate! Respond!

I hope that you have enjoyed reading this book. But don't get it twisted, this book is not just for entertainment. The purpose of this book is to save your life. After reading this book, you can't use the excuse "NO ONE TOLD ME". I'm telling you, and I will continue to tell you in books to come. I want to help you break down negative cycles, overcome traumatic experiences, endure peer pressure, resist temptation, and many other things that young people face today.

There will be times when you will question if it's all worth it. Fight through those feelings, keep in mind those things that end great, don't always start out great. What is your favorite dish? (wings? Fries? Pizza? Juicy burger? Cake?) Whatever it may be, when you think about those things, you picture the end results. Those end results smell and taste delicious, but if you go back to the very beginning when the process and preparation began, it's not so appetizing. Raw chicken, a dented dusty potato, raw ground beef, etc. Right now, you are that raw chicken wing and that dented potato, but with the right work and preparation, you will be just as desirable as any finished dish that you can think of. Nonetheless you need to ask yourself right now, am I putting the wrong ingredients in my recipe of life? The same thing will happen to you in life that will happen to your favorite dish, it won't turn out the way you want it to.

No, it won't be easy. So, don't be afraid to seek help when necessary. Have a plan in place for those difficult times. It's not a matter of if the temptation, pressure, frustration and other things will come, it's a matter of when it will come. Know that everyone is not your friend, understand that just because it's your family member, doesn't mean they can't be a bad influence.

Another thing to remember, staying busy with positive things will help keep negative things from entering your life, you won't have time for it. At the end of the day, it's not about what you have done prior to reading this book, it's about what you are going to do afterwards. Are you going to just close the book and continue down the wrong path? Or are you going to take control of your life and work to make it the life that you deserve? A life that you will be proud of and happy to live?

If it takes reading this book over and over again to help motivate and strengthen you, DO IT!! I want to help you to succeed in life, but I'm going to need you to do your part. With the help of you, me, and any other positive people in your life, you are going to be just fine, and that's REAL TALK.